P9-BIF-266

GAME BOY®
SECRET
CODES

//|||BRADYGAM
TAKE YOUR GAME F

GAME BOY®
SECRET CODES

LEGAL STUFF

Game Boy is a registered trademark of Nintendo of America Inc. ™, ® and the "N" logo are trademarks of Nintendo of America Inc. All rights reserved.

Brady Publishing
An Imprint of
Macmillan USA, Inc.
201 West 103rd Street
Indianapolis, Indiana 46290

ISBN: 1-56686-902-1

Library of Congress Catalog No.: 99-73007

Printing Code: The rightmost double-digit number is the year of the book's printing; the rightmost single-digit number is the number of the book's printing. For example, 99-1 shows that the first printing of the book occurred in 1999.

03 02 01 00   5

Manufactured in the United States of America.

Limits of Liability and Disclaimer of Warranty: THE AUTHOR AND PUBLISHER MAKE NO WARRANTY OF ANY KIND, EXPRESSED OR IMPLIED, WITH REGARD TO THESE PROGRAMS OR THE DOCUMENTATION CONTAINED IN THIS BOOK. THE AUTHOR AND PUBLISHER SPECIFICALLY DISCLAIM ANY WARRANTIES OF MERCHANTABILITY OR FITNESS FOR A PARTICULAR PURPOSE. THE AUTHOR AND PUBLISHER SHALL NOT BE LIABLE IN ANY EVENT FOR INCIDENTAL OR CONSEQUENTIAL DAMAGES IN CONNECTION WITH, OR ARISING OUT OF THE FURNISHING, PERFORMANCE, OR USE OF THE PROGRAMS.

BRADYGAMES STAFF

Publisher
Lynn Zingraf

Editor-In-Chief
H. Leigh Davis

Licensing Manager
David Waybright

Marketing Manager
Janet Eshenour

Acquisitions Editor
Debra McBride

Development Editor
David Cassady

Creative Director
Scott Watanabe

Marketing Assistant
Tricia Reynolds

CREDITS

Project Editor
Timothy Fitzpatrick

Screenshot Editor
Michael Owen

Book Designer
Kurt Owens

Production Designers
Jane Washburne
Bob Klunder

ACKNOWLEDGMENTS

BradyGAMES would like to thank
at Nintendo of America, especi
Loftus, Juana Tingdale, and
Testing Group. Without v
assistance and expert
this guide would n

BEAT MANIA GB

BATTLE

GAME LIST

GAME LIST

GAME LIST

GAME LIST

GAME LIST

GAME BOY® LEGEND

ABBREV.	WHAT IT MEANS
Left	Left on + Control Pad
Right	Right on + Control Pad
Down	Down on + Control Pad
Up	Up on + Control Pad
Start	Press Start button
Select	Press Select button
A	Press A Button
B	Press B Button

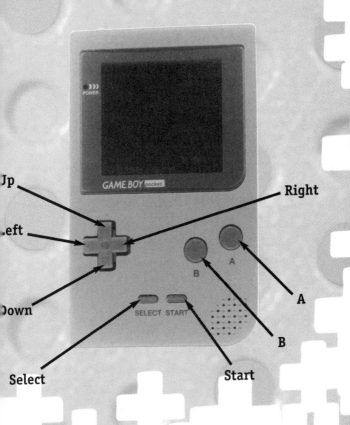

A BUG'S LIFE

PASSWORDS

LEVEL	PASSWORD
1	9LKK
2	BL26
3	5P9K
4	6652
5	BKK2
6	2PLB
7	6562
8	L59B
9	L59B
Bonus	BL26

THE ADDAMS FAMILY 2: PUGSLEY'S SCAVENGER HUNT

STATUS	PASSWORD
Rescued Granny	MP7VB
Rescued Gomez	MS5VB
Rescued Wednesday	M73VT
Rescued Uncle Fester	MH49K

ADVENTURE ISLAND

WORLD SELECT MODE

At the Title Screen, press **Right, Left, Right, Left, A, B, A, B.**

ADVENTURE ISLAND II

99 OF EVERYTHING

Enter the password **0894.**

AFTER BURST

LEVEL	PASSWORD
6	31520347
11	11145378
16	13020060
21	36985214
26	93493887

A
B
C
D
E
F
G
H
I
J
K
L
M
N
O
P
Q
R
S
T
U
V
W
X
Y
Z

ALADDIN

LEVEL SKIP

Pause the game and press **A, B, B, A, A, B, B, A.**

AMAR STORY

PASSWORDS

LEVEL	PASSWORD
1	LISUEURD
2	NINTENDO
3	ROBSONIC
4	OUTRUNST

AMAZING PENGUIN

ROOM	PASSWORD
1	678163
2	302945
3	152876
9	235403
13	678163
17	302945
21	153876
26	840492
29	054217
33	689721
37	916328

AMAZING TATER

COMPLETE ALL FLOORS
Enter the password **YBTF5ZZFT2**.

A
B
C
D
E
F
G
H
I
J
K
L
M
N
O
P
Q
R
S
T
U
V
W
X
Y
Z

ANIMANIACS

SCENES 1 AND 3 COMPLETE PASSWORD
Dot, Yako, Yako
Nothing, Yako, Dot
Dot, Dot, Wako

ASTEROIDS

CHEAT MENU
To enter the cheat menu, enter CHEATONX as your password, then press Select to enter the menu.

Level Select: Up or Down
Zone Select: Left or Right
"A" toggles invincibility

PASSWORDS
Zone 2: SPACEVAC
Zone 3: STARSBRN
Zone 4: WORMSIGN
Zone 5: INCOMING

CLASSIC ASTEROIDS

Enter QRTREATR as your password for the original '70s version of the game.

Unlock secret "Excalibur" spaceship.

Enter PROJECTX as your password for the secret ship.

THE ATOMIC PUNK

LEVEL 50 PASSWORD

Enter the password **B0MNDPBL3N CB3L2H2DJJ**.

AVENGING SPIRIT

TOUGHER GAME

At the Title Screen, press **Up + A + B**. You should hear a tone if done correctly.

LEVEL SKIP

Pause the game and press **A, B, B, A, A, B, A, A**.

A
B
C
D
E
F
G
H
I
J
K
L
M
N
O
P
Q
R
S
T
U
V
W
X
Y
Z

BATMAN

SOUND TEST

At the Title Screen, press **Up/Right** + **START**.

```
SOUND   TEST

SOUND   00

START A OR B
EXIT  SELECT

    SUNSOFT 1990
```

BATMAN FOREVER

CHEAT MODE

At the Difficulty Select Screen, press **Up, Right, Down, Left, Up, Left, Down, Right**.

CHEATS MENU:
>ALL AMMO:N
DAMAGE ON:Y
LEV START:1

BATTLE ARENA TOSHINDEN

ALL CHARACTERS

When Ellis starts dancing, press **Up, Down, B, A, Right, Left, B, A**.

FASTER CPU

At the Title Screen, press **Up, Up, Select, A, Up, Up, B**.

PLAY AS GAIA II OR SHO

At the Takara logo, press **SELECT** three times. When Ellis appears, press **Right, Left, A, B**.

VIEW CHARACTER SCREENS

At the Takara logo, press **B, A, Left, Right, B, A, Down, Up, B, A**.

SCORCHER MODE

At the Takara logo, press **SELECT** three times.

BATTLE BULL

PASSWORDS

LEVEL	PASSWORD
1	LK**
2	LP**
3	LT**
4	LZ**
5	L3**
6	L7**
7	L***
8	WF**
9	WK**
10	WP**
11	WT**
12	WZ**
13	W3**
14	W7**
15	W***
16	6F**
17	6K**
18	6P**

LEVEL	PASSWORD
19	6T**
20	6Z**

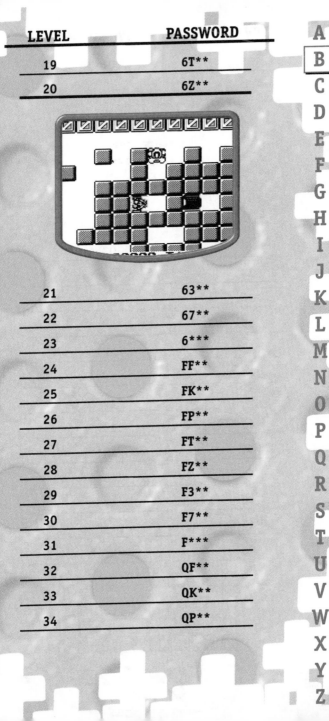

LEVEL	PASSWORD
21	63**
22	67**
23	6***
24	FF**
25	FK**
26	FP**
27	FT**
28	FZ**
29	F3**
30	F7**
31	F***
32	QF**
33	QK**
34	QP**

A
B
C
D
E
F
G
H
I
J
K
L
M
N
O
P
Q
R
S
T
U
V
W
X
Y
Z

LEVEL	PASSWORD
35	QT**

```
      REST 03
      STAGE 35
      BATTLE START
      TARGET
          COUNT 18
```

LEVEL	PASSWORD
36	QZ**
37	Q3**
38	Q7**
39	Q***
40	1F**
41	1K**
42	1P**
43	1T**
44	1Z**
45	13**
46	17**
47	1***
48	$F**

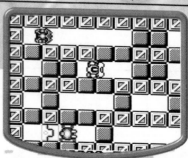

24

BATTLE PINGPONG

PASSWORDS

OPPONENT	PASSWORD
KRN	7822
CAN	6524
JPN	1604
URS	0781
USA	5802
SWE	8731
CHN	0511

STOP WATCH

Enter the password **1199**.

BATTLESHIP

PASSWORDS

STAGE	PASSWORD
2	QYBGTK
4	GKPQZP
5	QRKGTD
6	QPDGYM
7	QQLGTD
8	QXFGTL
9	QNMGTK
10	NPGGYM
11	NXHGTL
12	NQBGYD
13	NQZGPD
14	NNCGYK
15	HJXQCN

STAGE	PASSWORD
16	NYDGTK
17	NWLGTM
18	NTFGTB
19	NRMGTD
20	BBQQBP
21	YPHGTM
22	YRBGTD
23	YRZGXD
24	YQCGTD
25	YSKGPC
26	BCSQBV
27	BDVQJQ
28	YYFGPK
29	BJRQZN
30	TRGGTD
31	JDNQJQ
32	TXBGTL
33	ZKTQKP
34	ZHPQCW
35	JCXQJV
36	TVDGTL
37	TTLGPB
38	JZWQKX
39	JMRQCQ
40	PXGGTL
41	CHNQBW
42	CGYQJS
43	CDTQZQ
44	CBPQBP
45	CMXQCQ
46	CKSQJP
47	CLVQZV
48	PPFGYM
End	PQMGTD

BATTLE UNIT ZEOTH

VIEW LEVEL

At the Title Screen when the music stops, press **A + B + Down**. You should hear a tone if done correctly. Do this twice to view level 2, three times for level 3, etc.

BEAT MANIA GB

EXTRA SONGS

Enter the following passwords for extra songs in Free Mode:

PASSWORD	SONGS
RELAXATION	Classic 3, e.n.k.
REMIX	Big beat mix
FEVER	disco
SENSE	disco, big beat mix
VISUAL	eurobeat, big beat mix
MOTHER	e.n.k., disco

D.J. BATTLE

Enter **BEATMANIA**, **KONAMI**, or **KCEK** to play Dj battle on Free Mode.

BEAVIS & BUTTHEAD

PASSWORDS

LEVEL	PASSWORD
2	PTRSR
3	FTGBR
3	RLPDV
4	ZPQNL
5	VXJCD
6	FKLTM

BILL AND TED'S EXCELLENT ADVENTURE

PASSWORDS

LEVEL	PASSWORD
2	555-4239
3	555-6767
4	555-8942

LEVEL	PASSWORD
5	555-4118
6	555-8471
7	555-2989
8	555-6737
9	555-6429
10	555-1881

A
B
C
D
E
F
G
H
I
J
K
L
M
N
O
P
Q
R
S
T
U
V
W
X
Y
Z

BIONIC COMMANDO

FINAL BOSS

Enter the following password where S=Square, T=Triangle, B=Ball:

	A	B	C	D	E	F
1	S	B	S	S	B	B
2	T	S	_	T	S	B
3	T	S	B	_	T	B
4	B	T	_	B	B	T

GOOD LUCK

RE-EQUIP

Hold **START** and press **A + B**.

BLACK BASS

FISH BOTH LAKES

At the Password Screen, enter **K** in each space.

BLADES OF STEEL

SOUND TEST

At the Ultra Games Screen, press **Up, Up, Down, Down, Left, Right, Left, Right, B, A, B, A, START**.

BLASTER MASTER BOY

PERIOD SELECT

At the Title Screen, highlight Continue, hold **A** and press **START**.

A
B
C
D
E
F
G
H
I
J
K
L
M
N
O
P
Q
R
S
T
U
V
W
X
Y
Z

BLODIA

WARM UP PASSWORDS

LEVEL	PASSWORD
16	AIJD
17	DIFP
19	DJGN
20	BKQF
21	ANPD

LEVEL	PASSWORD
21	CNGL
22	APQD
23	DQMQ
24	BNCE
25	CPHI

BOMBERMAN GB

ONE-PLAYER BATTLE MODE
Enter the password **5656**.

ATOMIC DETONATOR
Enter the password **5151**.

SOUND TEST
Enter the password **2145**.

ALL POWER-UPS
Enter the password **4622**.

PASSWORDS

LEVEL	PASSWORD
2	9634
3	1637
4	0320
5	6524
6	3260
7	4783
8	5472

BOOMER'S ADVENTURE IN SMIK WORLD

LEVEL SELECT
Enter the password **ANCIENT**.

A
B
C
D
E
F
G
H
I
J
K
L
M
N
O
P
Q
R
S
T
U
V
W
X
Y
Z

BUBBLE BOBBLE

ROUND 100

Enter the password **KGLJ**.

BUBBLE BOBBLE JUNIOR

STAGE SELECT

Enter **Right Arrow, 5, Right Arrow, V** as your password. Press **START** to get to the Round Select Screen. Use **Up** and **Down** to cycle through the rounds and press **START** to begin.

BUGS BUNNY'S CRAZY CASTLE 2

PASSWORDS

LEVEL	PASSWORD
2	TEST
3	GAME
4	SHIP
5	RACE
6	WORD
7	SHOP
8	SIZE
9	QUIZ
10	DOLL
11	DATE
12	ZOOM
13	DISK
14	MOLD
15	ZERO
16	FIRE
17	ROOT
18	READ
19	TAPE
20	UNIT
21	SONG
22	TYRE
23	LOVE
24	NOTE
25	JAZZ
26	HELP
27	KING
28	GIFT

BUGS BUNNY CRAZY CASTLE 3

PASSWORDS

LEVEL	PASSWORD
4	SXBX47
5	XCB84R
6	CTB84R
7	CSB8G7
8	TXB24H
9	1SB849
10	LCB8GW
11	5TBV4R
12	OLB84W
14	81BV47
15	45B2G7
16	GLBVG7
17	QLBVGW
18	?5BVGW
19	MDBX4K
20	30B84K
21	NOB8BB
22	28B8G2
23	R4B8G2
24	HGB24V
25	7MBXGZ
26	W3B8G6
27	JNBX4K
28	92B249
60	97X3GW

BURGER TIME DELUXE

PASSWORDS

LEVEL	PASSWORD
2-1	Egg, Egg, Hot Dog, Mr. Pepper
3-1	Hot Dog, Mr. Pepper, Mr. Pepper, Pickle
4-1	Pickle, Egg, Egg, Pickle
5-1	Tomato, Tomato, Pickle, Mr. Pepper
6-1	Pickle, Tomato, Tomato, Hot Dog

BUST-A-MOVE 4

EXTRA PUZZLES

At the Title Screen, press **A, Left, Right, Left, A.** A figure should appear in the lower right corner.

EXTRA CHARACTERS

At the main menu, press **Up, Down, Left, Left, Right, Up, A, B, B, A.**

CASTLEVANIA II: BELMONT'S REVENGE

PASSWORDS

LEVEL	PASSWORD
Central Castle	Heart, Ball, Candle, Space

Belmont's Son	Heart, Candle, Ball, Ball
Count Dracula	Ball, Heart, Candle, Heart
Easier Game	Candle, Candle, Heart, Heart
Harder Game	Space, Ball, Space, Ball
Sound Test	Heart, Heart, Heart, Heart

CASTLEVANIA LEGENDS

STANDARD MODE PASSWORDS

STAGE	PASSWORD
2	Axe, Axe, Space, Knife
3	Axe, Cross, Space, Candle
4	Watch, Space, Knife, Meat

STAGE	PASSWORD
5-1	Watch, Holy Water, Meat, Candle
5-2	Knife, Candle, Candle, Candle
Bonus	Knife, Space, Candle, Meat

LIGHT MODE PASSWORDS

LEVEL	PASSWORD
2	Cross, Axe, Axe, Watch
3	Cross, Cross, Space, Meat
4	Candle, Axe, Watch, Candle
5-1	Candle, Holy Water, Meat, Meat
5-2	Meat, Candle, Candle, Meat
Bonus	Meat, Space, Meat, Candle

SUPER PASSWORD

Enter the password **Meat, Candle, Candle, Meat.**

A
B
C
D
E
F
G
H
I
J
K
L
M
N
O
P
Q
R
S
T
U
V
W
X
Y
Z

CAT TRAP

LEVEL 100

Enter the password **R61H**.

CHASE HQ

LEVEL SELECT

At the Title Screen, hold **Down + A + B** and press **START**.

CHOPLIFTER II

PASSWORDS

LEVEL	CODE
1-2	SKYHPPR
1-3	LKYBYSS
2-1	CHPLFTR

2-2	BYMSFWR
2-3	RGHTHND
3-1	GDGMPLY
3-2	TRYHRDR
3-3	SPRYSKS
4-1	CMPTRWZ

LEVEL	CODE
4-2	CHPYBYS
4-3	VRYHPPY
5-1	GMBYQZD
5-2	LVLYTYZ
5-3	GDDYGMZ

A
B
C
D
E
F
G
H
I
J
K
L
M
N
O
P
Q
R
S
T
U
V
W
X
Y
Z

COLLEGE SLAM

BONUS PLAYERS

At the Title Screen, press **B, B, A, A, B, B, A, B, A, B, B, A, B, SELECT, B, SELECT, A, SELECT**.

BONUS TEAMS

At the Title Screen, press **A, A, B, A, B, A, B, B, A, B, A, SELECT**.

BETTER SKILLS

At the Tonight's Match-Up Screen, press **A, A, A, A, B, B, B, A, B, A, B, A, B + SELECT**.

DISPLAY SHOT PERCENTAGE

At the Tonight's Match-Up Screen, press **Down, B, Up, Up, Down**.

IMPROVED THREE-POINTERS

At the Tonight's Match-Up Screen, press **B, B, A, A, B, A, B, B, A, B, A, A**.

CONTRA: THE ALIEN WARS

INFINITE LIVES

Enter the password **B32R**.

LEVEL SKIP

Enter the password **H2F2**. Press **START** during the game to skip a level.

PASSWORDS

LEVEL	PASSWORD
2	3KNT
3	MDWH
4	2S3W
5	1Z5C

COSMO TANK

SOUND TEST

On the subscreen at the beginning of the Quest Mode, simultaneously press and hold **Down + A + B**. While holding these, press **START**. If this is done correctly, the message "Sound Test 01" will appear.

CRASH TEST DUMMIES

CHEAT MODE

At the Title Screen, press **Up, Down, Left, Right**.

TWO PLAYER

At the Title Screen, press **SELECT, SELECT, START**.

DAFFY DUCK: THE MARVIN MISSIONS

PASSWORDS

STAGE	PASSWORD
1	72308
3	04070
4	82048

WEAPON SELECT

Defeat ten enemies, pause the game, and enter the following:

ITEM	CODE
Laser	Up, Up
Big Bullet	Down, Down
Bouncing	Left, Left
Rapid Fire	Right, Right
Health Refill	B, B
No Change	SELECT

DEAD HEAT SCRAMBLE

STAGE SELECT

At the Title Screen, press **B (x8), A (x8), B (one less time than the stage you want)**. For example, if you want Stage 10, press **B (x8), A (x8), B (x9)**. Press **START** to begin.

```
        STAGE10
  RATE    0060000
  TIME    1:20:00
```

DICK TRACEY

PASSWORDS

LEVEL	PASSWORD
2	49730
3	64608
4	59715
5	56115

DONKEY KONG LAND 2

40 BANANA COINS

At the Game Selection Screen, highlight your game, hold **Right or Left**, and press **B, B, A, A.** You should hear a sound if entered correctly.

ALL KREMCOINS

At the Game Selection Screen, highlight your game, hold **Right or Left**, and press **A, B, A, B.** You should hear a sound if entered correctly.

EXTRA LIVES

At the Game Selection Screen, highlight your game, hold **Right or Left**, and press **A, A, B, B.** You should hear a sound if entered correctly.

THE LOST WORLD

Collect all 47 Kremcoins.

DONKEY KONG LAND 3

INFINITE LIVES

At the Title Screen, press **Down, Down, Up, Left, Right**.

MATCHING CARD GAME

At the Title Screen, press **Up, Up, Down, Left, Right**. Press **START** to play the game.

DRAGON BALL Z 2

MINI-GAME

At the Title Screen, press **Up, Down, Left, Right, Down, Up, Right, Left, A**.

DRAGONHEART

PASSWORDS

LEVEL	PASSWORD
2	BCDLST
3	DCLTSB
4	LCTBSD
5	CBLSBT
6	TTSCDC
7	SDCDTS
8	BVDVSC

ELEVATOR ACTION

? DOORS

Enter a ? Door with the following digits in the hundred spot on your score to get the item:

DIGIT	ITEM
1 or 2	Shotgun
3 or 4	Machinegun
5 or 6	Pistol
6 or 7	Grenade
8 or 9	Heart

F-15 STRIKE EAGLE

PILOTCODES

LEVEL	PILOTCODE
2	FH1D6390

3	911F638D
4	441H6348
5	H01H63BD
6	C31J63C8
7	7D10637B
8	F71073B3

A
B
C
D
E
F
G
H
I
J
K
L
M
N
O
P
Q
R
S
T
U
V
W
X
Y
Z

LEVEL	PILOTCODE
9	80217365
10	072173FH
11	BD2273CD
12	5F237376
13	JG23730F
14	B12473C1
15	3H257317
16	9725736B
17	31267343
18	F72673B9
19	5J277374
20	062773F9

FINAL FANTASY LEGEND

SOUND TEST

At the Title Screen, hold **Down + SELECT + A** for about five seconds.

FINAL FANTASY LEGEND II

SOUND TEST

At the Title Screen, hold **SELECT + B + START**.

FIST OF THE NORTH STAR

LAST LEVEL

Enter the password **XKP 72QN VHR JGU5**.

FOREMAN FOR REAL

PASSWORDS

BOUT	PASSWORD
Janetti vs. Jones	FKBKFGKD
Janetti vs. Foreman	FKBBGGKP

FROGGER

STOP TRAFFIC AND TURTLES.

Press A, B, B, Left, Right, Up, B, A during gameplay. If done properly, a traffic light should appear and stop all traffic, and turtles will no longer dive underwater.

CHEAT MODE

After losing all of your lives, press A, B, Select, Start at the High Score screen.

GARGOYLE'S QUEST

PASSWORDS

LEVEL	PASSWORD
2	MUPP-JMHW
3	GJ7Q-KLVO
4	SWXE-CBFJ
5	BIF8-BRAZ
6	FWGG-57CY
7	HWTL-90AZ
8	N5AQ-9RZF
End	WPXF-4BDQ

A B C D E F G H I J K L M N O P Q R S T U V W X Y Z

GEX: ENTER THE GECKO

ALL REMOTES

Enter the following password by holding the indicated button and pressing the direction at each spot. **B + Down (x20), B + Up, A + Right, A + Left (x2), B + Down (x2), B + Right, A + Right**

255 LIVES

To max out your lives remaining instantly, follow these steps:

A: Enter a stage with a bottomless pit with one life remaining.

B: Fall down the pit.

C: As the "fall over dead" animation is playing, exit the level through the pause menu.

D: Repeat steps A-C and you should have 255 lives. However, you will have to get a Red remote from ANOTHER stage to be able to receive a valid password.

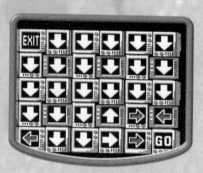

GO! GO! TANK

EXTRA TANKS

At the Title Screen, press **Left, Up, Right, Up, Left, Left, Up, Right, Up, Left, Up, Right, START**.

INVINCIBILITY

At the Title Screen, press **Left, Up, Right, Up, Left, Left, Up, Right, Up, Left, Up, Left, START**.

A
B
C
D
E
F
G
H
I
J
K
L
M
N
O
P
Q
R
S
T
U
V
W
X
Y
Z

GODZILLA

PASSWORDS

LEVEL	PASSWORD
2	GL6T
3	C47?
4	8W2H
5	WT7Q
6	B#QGGH4/
7	39TN
8	JHJ/
9	=M3K
10	T94/
11	HB2/
12	1XPK
13	71CL
14	C?#2
15	GG1C
16	?KGQ9T4M
17	L&=7
18	SC/W
19	Q41M
20	8QH=
21	=65=
22	T8CJ
23	?7QG
24	LC/W
25	?=5Q
26	MXRT
End	JXRB7K&948HPD32#JN

SOUND TEST

At the Title Screen, press **A, B, SELECT** to access the Sound Test Menu.

HARVEST MOON

FREE EGGS

To get free eggs, buy a chicken and, during the same year, take an egg after it has been laid. Hurl the egg against the wall; it will become stuck in the wall. Use your sickle to cut the egg from the wall and stick it in a shipping box. Now cut another egg out the same way. You should be able to acquire nearly 100 eggs from a single one in this fashion.

SELL EGGS AT CHICKEN RATES

Take an egg one of your chickens has produced and put it into an incubator. Walk to the animal store with it and select **Sell Chicken**, but highlight your incubating egg. The store owner will purchase the egg and pay the full price for an actual chicken.

HERCULES

PASSWORDS

LEVEL	PASSWORD
2	B7FG4
3	XTV5P
4	TV5DP
5	FX6NL
6	HGRSV
7	K7DGR
8	FTXCG
9	GSJ4H

CREDITS

Enter the password **CRDTS**.

HOME ALONE

FINAL LEVEL WITH ALL ITEMS

At the Title Screen press **Up, Down, Right, Left, SELECT**.

HONG KONG

SOUND TEST

Press **B + START** at the second screen of the game.

TEST MODE

Press **A + B + START** at the second screen of the game.

VIEW ENDING

Press **A + START** at the second screen of the game.

THE HUMANS

PASSWORDS

LEVEL	PASSWORD
3	QWSD
5	MNBV
9	PYST
21	SSXC

HUNT FOR RED OCTOBER

EXTRA FUEL

Hold **A + B**, then press **SELECT, Left, Right** when the sub course is displayed.

EXTRA MISSILES

Hold **A + B**, then press **Up, Down** when the sub course is displayed.

EXTRA SHIPS

Hold **A + B**, then press **SELECT, Up, Down** when the sub course is displayed.

LEVEL SELECT

At the Main Screen press **B, SELECT, Left, Right, START**.

HYPER LODE RUNNER

LEVEL SELECT

Enter the password **QM-0388**.

INDIANA JONES AND THE LAST CRUSADE

PASSWORDS

LEVEL	PASSWORD
3	D912H4133D
4	0313B51330

IRON MAN/X-O MANOWAR IN HEAVY METAL

PASSWORDS

LEVEL	PASSWORD
1	TYCKPQ
2	TJYPDF
3	ZXCVBM
4	KDZCPL
5	MGHQZS
6	SPLHRJ
7	YPMBCK
8	SDWZCM
9	DPWMQZ
10	LKLPDX
11	XCSQSS
12	MPQPRY
13	JKRTSC
14	DXCMGH
15	LPJKHX
16	XCSMMN
17	VNTMZS
18	SXZPLK
19	MPKHKG
20	BMQZHL

JAMES BOND 007

BONUS GAMES

Enter your name as one of the following:

NAME	GAME
BJACK	Black Jack

NAME	GAME
BACCR	Baccarat
REDOG	Red Dog

JUDGE DREDD

LEVEL SELECT

At the Title Screen, press **A, Left, Right, B, START**.

PASSWORD

LEVEL	PASSWORD
4	ANDERSON

A
B
C
D
E
F
G
H
I
J
K
L
M
N
O
P
Q
R
S
T
U
V
W
X
Y
Z

THE JUNGLE BOOK

CHEAT MODE

During gameplay, press **SELECT** to access the Options. Select Music/Effects, and play the following sounds in order: **40, 30, 20, 19, 18, 17, 16, 15.**

JUNGLE STRIKE

PASSWORDS

LEVEL	PASSWORD
2	4975200968
3	2922502918
4	6505068908
5	0540524815
6	0550792954
7	0950035298
8	0155908131
9	1185402550

JURASSIC PARK

LEVEL SKIP

As the Options are revealed, press **Up, Down, Left, Up, Down, Right, SELECT**. Repeat this step again, and you should hear an explosion. During your game, pause and press **SELECT**.

KID DRACULA

PASSWORDS

LEVEL	PASSWORD
2	5613
3	3272
4	7283
5	5346
6	7225
7	5539
8	7158

KILLER INSTINCT

LEVEL SELECT

At the Title Screen, **hold Up and press A, B, START**.

PLAY AS EYEDOL

At the Versus Screen, **hold Right and press SELECT, START, B, A**.

RANDOM SELECT

Hold **Up and press START** at the Player Selection Screen.

KIRBY'S DREAM LAND

CONTINUE

At the Title Screen, press **Up + SELECT + A**.

CHEAT MENU

At the Title Screen, press **Down + SELECT + B**.

HARDER GAME

At the Title Screen, press **Up + SELECT + B**.

KIRBY'S PINBALL LAND

BONUS GAMES

At the Title Screen, press **Left + B + SELECT**. A white cat should walk past the Ranking Screen. Begin a new game to play the bonus game.

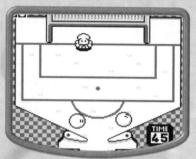

BOSS SELECT

At the Title Screen, **hold Right and press A + B + SELECT**. A black cat should walk past the Ranking Screen.

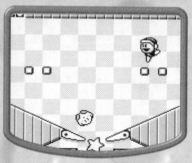

KLAX (COLOR GAME BOY)

MINI GAME

Enter the password **Green Alien, Green Alien, Circle, Square.**

KNIGHT'S QUEST

FINAL PASSWORD

Enter **mn7nB dc!Zc SHhh&** as the password.

KRUSTY'S FUN HOUSE

PASSWORDS

LEVEL	PASSWORD
2	MC BAIN
3	MILHOUSE
4	CMBURNS
5	PRINCESS

THE LEGEND OF ZELDA: LINK'S AWAKENING

ALTERNATE MUSIC

Start a new player and enter your name as **ZELDA**.

SAVE YOUR MONEY

To save money on those big purchases such as the Bow, carry an item to the counter and as the money starts to drain, immediately press **Select+Start+A+B** to go to the save menu. Select "Save and Quit," then re-load your game. Depending on how fast you were, some or even most of your money should be left and the game won't take what remains.

LION KING

LEVEL SKIP

Pause the game and press **B, A, A, B, A, A**.

LOCK 'N' CHASE

EXTRA LEVELS

At the Title Screen, press **A, A, B, B, A, B, B**.

LOONEY TUNES: TWOUBLE
PASSWORDS

LEVEL	PASSWORD
Granny's House	Dog, Granny, Tweety, Taz, Sylvester
Granny's Cellar	Taz, Sylvester, Tweety, Dog, Granny
Garden	Sylvester, Tweety, Dog, Taz, Granny
Out in the Streets	Dog, Tweety, Taz, Granny, Sylvester
Toy Shop	Taz, Dog, Tweety, Sylvester, Granny

LOST WORLD: JURASSIC PARK
PASSWORDS

LEVEL	PASSWORD
2	KQTV
3	NPLX
4	BGMD
5	HRTY
6	JFCD
7	MRBM
8	XGNT

LUCKY LUKE
PASSWORDS

LEVEL	PASSWORD
1	Luke, Horse, Horse, Old Man, Luke
2	Coyote, Horse, Luke, Old Man, Old Man
3	Old Man, Coyote, Luke, Horse, Coyote
4	Coyote, Horse, Luke, Old Man, Coyote

MARIO CLASH

LEVEL SKIP

While playing press **Left, Left, Left, Right, Left, Right, Left, Left**.

MARIO GOLF

EARN 300 EXPERIENCE

If you find the other three characters, you earn 30 experience. You can't find the character you are playing as. The following are the locations of each character.

CHARACTER	LOCATION
Sherry	Northern most part of Tiny Tots
Azalea	Rightmost part of Palm's Putting Groun▸
Joe	Leftmost part of Raven Woods
Kid	In the tree by the entrance to the Links Club Putting Range

LEFT-HANDED

Hold the Select Button as you select your characte▸ in order to play left-handed. This doesn't work with Sherry, Azalea, Joe, or Kid.

LEVEL UP MUSHROOMS

One is on the bookshelf in the room to the right o▸ the director's room. The second is in the cabinet ir▸ the club maker's hut. Look in the bushes to the lef▸ of where you arrive at Peach's Castle for the third.

PEACH'S CASTLE COURSE

Win all four tournaments and beat each club's pro▸

UNLOCK PUTTS, GRACE, TINY, GENE YUSS

Speak to the character in the lounge that you wish to open up. Defeat him or her to play as that character.

UNLOCK WARIO

Defeat the club pros and tournaments.

MEGA MAN 3

FINAL STAGE PASSWORD

Enter the password **A0, B0, C1, C2, B2.**

MEGA MAN 4

ULTIMATE PASSWORD

Enter the following password:

```
_ _ R R B _
_ E _ R E _
B _ _ _ E _
_ B R _ _ B
```

MEGA MAN 5

PASSWORD

Enter the following password:

```
R R T _ _
E T _ _ T
_ E _ R T
T T R R E
T R T R R
```

MEN IN BLACK: THE SERIES

FLY

Enter the password **0601.** This should give you an error. During the game, hold **SELECT + Up** to fly. Hold **SELECT + A** to get more firepower.

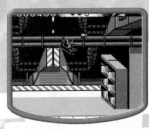

PASSWORDS

LEVEL	PASSWORD
2	2710
3	1807
4	0309
5	2705
6	3107
Ending	1943

Thanks Slick, but we need the LTD looking like new...

STAGE SKIP

Enter the password **2409**. It should give you an error. While playing, pause the game and press **SELECT** to skip to the next level.

Aliens are on the rampage through the streets of Manhattan...

MERCENARY FORCE

50,000 YEN

At the Title Screen, **hold Up + SELECT + A + B and press START**.

STAGE SELECT

After entering the *50,000 Yen* code (above), press **START**. When Round 1 appears, press **Right** to change the stage. Press **START** to begin.

METROID II: RETURN OF SAMUS

REFILL MISSILE SUPPLY AND HEALTH

Inside your ship, walk against the left wall to refill your health and the right wall for your missile supply.

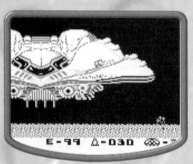

MICKEY MOUSE MAGIC WANDS

PASSWORDS

STAGE	PASSWORD
2	BVCK
3	FXLL
4	GRWN
5	WHVT
6	BZSS
7	CZCK
8	DRWP
9	BXLK
10	HWNT
Boss 1	SLVP
11	SPZT

STAGE	PASSWORD
12	BLZW
13	GRWP
14	TRVP
15	BWLL
16	WVLK
17	DRZP
18	FLVG
19	HZST
20	TQPY
Boss 2	JXMP
21	MQLT
22	FRYT
23	RQNT
24	LQST
25	JXRY
26	MQND
27	SQLL
28	TWCK
29	NWCK
30	SZFT
Boss 3	PQCK
31	YVRD
32	RQST
33	SZLD
34	FRZM
35	THVN
36	CQNT
37	PZST
38	HQRS
39	SWLK
40	CHWP
Boss 4	JZWL

A
B
C
D
E
F
G
H
I
J
K
L
M
N
O
P
Q
R
S
T
U
V
W
X
Y
Z

MIGHTY MORPHIN POWER RANGERS

PASSWORDS

LEVEL	PASSWORD
2	1001
3	1012
4	0175
5	1387

MIGHTY MORPHIN POWER RANGERS: THE MOVIE

PASSWORDS

Ivan Ooze	0411
Pig	5989
Rat	0936
Goldar	3713
Lord Zedd	3500

MONSTER MAX

PASSWORDS

LEVEL	PASSWORD
4	-8?-35R-
5	273?35RZ
6	JZVHMV3D
7	L5VP79N7
8	PL1H17P-
9	MQLYTY2D
10	-J#X5DKP

MONTEZUMA'S RETURN

UNLIMITED LIVES
Enter the password **ELEPHANT**.

UNLOCK ALL DOORS
Enter the password **SUNSHINE**.

FINAL BOSS
Enter the password **6JYBSPPJ**.

MORTAL KOMBAT 3

KOMBAT KODES
Enter these codes at the Vs. Screen:

CODE	EFFECT
100-100	Disable Throws
205-205	Fight Smoke

CODE	EFFECT
192-234	Play as Smoke

CODE	EFFECT
707-000	Player 1 at 1/4 energy
000-707	Player 2 at 1/4 energy
033-000	Player 1 at 1/2 energy
000-033	Player 2 at 1/2 energy
460-460	Randper Kombat
688-422	Dark Kombat
987-666	Message
123-926	Message

```
THERE IS NO
KNOWLEDGE THAT
IS NOT POWER
```

CODE	EFFECT
985-125	Pyscho Kombat
020-020	Blocking Disabled
987-123	No Powerbars

MORTAL KOMBAT 4

KOMBAT KODES

Enter the following codes at the Vs. Screen:

EFFECT	CODE
Enable Reptile	192-234

Fight Reptile	205-205

Throwing Disabled	100-100
Dark Kombat	688-422
Psycho Kombat	985-125
Explosive Kombat	050-050
Multiple Weapons	555-555
Noob Saibot Mode	012-012
Programmer Message	987-666
Programmer Msg. 2	123-926

EFFECT	CODE
Silent Kombat	666-666
Random Weapon	222-222
Switcheroo	460-460
Weapons Won't Be Dropped	002-002
Big Heads	321-321
Max Damage Disabled	010-010
Throws Disabled	100-100
Max Dam/Throw Disabled	110-110
Blocking Disabled	020-020
Computer Player Quarter Power	000-707
Computer Player Half Power	000-033
Human Player Quarter Power	707-000
Human Player Half Power	033-000
One Hit Wins	123-123
Randper Kombat	333-333

MULAN
PASSWORDS

LEVEL	PASSWORD
2	JSFPW
3	QGHXB

MYSTERIUM
LEVEL DROP

Press **SELECT** and choose the Map.
Press **B + SELECT + Down**.

PASS KEY

Press **SELECT** and choose the Map.
Press **A + B + Left + START**. You should now have a Pass Key. Drop this into a pool, and it will transform into a Downlevl. Drop the Downlevl into a pool, and it will transform into an Uplevel. Drop the Uplevel into a pool, and it will transform into a Superpow.

A B C D E F G H I J K L M N O P Q R S T U V W X Y Z

FILL UP INVENTORY

Press **SELECT** and choose the Map. Press **B + Up + SELECT**.

NBA JAM '99

CHAMPIONSHIP GAME

Select Playoffs and enter **MIK** as the initials. Then enter **R4QKFCWCDG** as the password.

NEMESIS

FULL WEAPONS AND SHIELDS

Pause the game and press **Up, Up, Down, Down, Left, Right, Left, Right, B, A, START.**

NO POWER-UPS

Pause the game and press **Up, SELECT, Down, SELECT, Left, SELECT, Right, SELECT, SELECT, SELECT, START**.

POWER DOWN

Pause the game and press **A, Left, Left, Left, Left, Left, START**.

SPEED AND SHIELDS

Pause the game and press **B, B, B, B, B, A, A, A, A, A**.

NFL BLITZ

CHEAT CODES

Enter the following codes at the Match-Up Screen. The first number is how many times you press **START**. The second number is how many times you press **B**. The third number is how many times you press **A**. Then press the direction indicated at the end of the code.

CODE	EFFECT
2,0,2 Right	Brick field
2,2,2 Right	Night game
3,2,3 Down	Parking lot
5,5,1 Up	Predator Mode
0,0,6 Up	Overtime
5,1,4 Up	Infinite turbos

4,3,3 Up	Invisible receiver
3,3,3 Left	No pointer

4,2,3 Down	No fumbles

PLAY AS EMERYSVILLE ECLIPSE
Enter the password **00606744**.

PLAY AS MIDWAY BLITZERS
Enter the password **06267545**.

NINJA BOY

STAGE SELECT

At the Title Screen, press **Up, Up, Down, Down, A, B, A, B.** Then **hold A and press START.** Press **Up or Down** to change the stage number. Press **START** to begin.

NINJA GAIDEN SHADOW

SOUND TEST

At the Title Screen, **hold A + B and press START.**

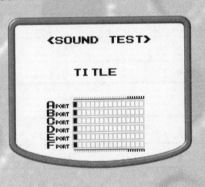

NINTENDO WORLD CUP

PASSWORDS

Select a match and team below, and combine the numbers for the password.

MATCH	CODE
Match 2	224—
Match 3	033—
Match 4	530—
Match 5	363—
Match 6	172—
Match 7	429—
Match 8	561—
Match 9	513—
Match 10	971—
Match 11	086—
Match 12	016—

TEAM	CODE
U.S.A.	—-31
Holland	—-41
Japan	—-59
France	—-26
Cameroon	—-54
U.S.S.R.	—-17
Mexico	—-72

TEAM	CODE
England	—-45
Spain	—-38
Brazil	—-51
Germany	—-13
Argentina	—-62
Italy	—-33

ODDWORLD ADVENTURES
PASSWORDS

PASSWORD	DOORS OPEN
JCBCM	1
JCCCL	1,7
SCBCC	1,2
JDBCL	1,3
JFBCP	1,4
JHBCR	1,5
JMBCC	1,6
SCCCB	1,2,7
SDBCB	1,2,3
JDCCM	1,3,7
JFCCN	1,4,7
JMCCB	1,6,7
JHCCQ	1,5,7

A
B
C
D
E
F
G
H
I
J
K
L
M
N
O
P
Q
R
S
T
U
V
W
X
Y
Z

PASSWORD	DOORS OPEN
JGBCN	1,3,4
JJBCQ	1,3,5
JNBCB	1,3,6
JKBCT	1,4,5
JPBCF	1,4,6
JRBCH	1,5,6

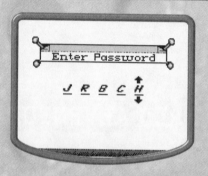

SHBCH	1,2,5
SFBCF	1,2,4
SMBCM	1,2,6
SDCCC	1,2,3,7
SFCCD	1,2,4,7
SHCCG	1,2,5,7
SMCCL	1,2,6,7
SGBCD	1,2,3,4
SJBCG	1,2,3,5
SNBCL	1,2,3,6
JRCCG	1,5,6,7

PASSWORD	DOORS OPEN
JPCCD	1,4,6,7
JNCCC	1,3,6,7
JKCCS	1,4,5,7
JJCCR	1,3,5,7
JGCCP	1,3,4,7
JLBCS	1,3,4,5
JQBCD	1,3,4,6
JSBCG	1,3,5,6
JTBCK	1,4,5,6
SRBCR	1,2,5,6
SKBCK	1,2,4,5
SPBCP	1,2,4,6
SNCCM	1,2,3,6,7
SGCCF	1,2,3,4,7
SJCCH	1,2,3,5,7
SKCCJ	1,2,4,5,7
SPCCN	1,2,4,6,7
SRCCQ	1,2,5,6,7
SLBCJ	1,2,3,4,5
SQBCN	1,2,3,4,6
SSBCQ	1,2,3,5,6
JTCCJ	1,4,5,6,7
JSCCH	1,3,5,6,7
JQCCF	1,3,4,6,7
JLCCT	1,3,4,5,7

A
B
C
D
E
F
G
H
I
J
K
L
M
N
O
P
Q
R
S
T
U
V
W
X
Y
Z

PASSWORD	DOORS OPEN
JBBCJ	1,3,4,5,6
STBCT	1,2,4,5,6
SSCCR	1,2,3,5,6,7
STCCS	1,2,4,5,6,7
SLCCK	1,2,3,4,5,7
SQCCP	1,2,3,4,6,7
SBBCS	1,2,3,4,5,6
JBCCK	1,3,4,5,6,7
SBCCT	all

BIG DOOR PASSWORDS

PASSWORD	PART
TBCCS	2nd Part
TBHCN	3rd Part
TBRCD	4th Part
TBRDF	5th Part
TBTBT	6th Part

OFF ROAD CHALLENGE

HIDDEN VEHICLES

At the Vehicle Select Screen, press the following buttons:

VEHICLE	CODE
The Crusher	Right-C
Toyota 4x4 Monster	Up-C
Thunder Bolt	Left-C
The Punisher	Down-C

OPERATION C

10 LIVES

At the Title Screen, press **Up (x4), Down (x4), Left (x4), START**.

LEVEL SELECT

At the Title Screen, press **Up, Up, Down, Down, Left, Right, Left, Right, B, A, B, A, START**.

SOUND TEST

At the Title Screen, press **Up, Down, Left, Right, START**.

PENGUIN WARS

LEVEL SELECT

At the Character Select Screen, **hold Left + B and press A**. Press Up or Down to select the level.

PIPE DREAM

PASSWORDS

STAGE	CODE
5	HAHA
9	GRIN
13	REAP
17	SEED
21	GROW
25	TALL
29	YALI

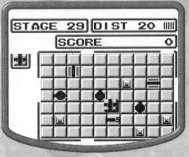

PITFALL: BEYOND THE JUNGLE

PASSWORDS

LEVEL	PASSWORD
Underground	FLTYWTRS
Volcano	GNGDWN

The Volcano

Prison	SLTHHRNG
The Scourge	SWPNGBLW

A
B
C
D
E
F
G
H
I
J
K
L
M
N
O
P
Q
R
S
T
U
V
W
X
Y
Z

POCAHONTAS

PASSWORDS

LEVEL	PASSWORD
2	KPGXH4T8
3	CMQZB6R1
4	JWDLF7K5
5	TGNDX3V9
6	HFSBD2M6
7	QZJRL1W4
8	BPXCV7Z3
9	SDLFT8G2
10	RWHJX9Z5
11	MVNGB4C6
12	KCQTD3W1
13	TBPRG5H8
14	QFCMX2B9
15	VDHKS6L7
16	BNJHZ1R9

POCKET BOMBERMAN

ALL POWER-UPS

Enter the password **4622**.

ALL ITEMS

Enter the password **5656**.

PASSWORDS

FOREST WORLD

AREA	PASSWORD
1	7693
2	3905
3	2438
4	8261
Boss	1893

OCEAN WORLD

AREA	PASSWORD
1	2805
2	9271

3	1354
4	4915
Boss	8649

A
B
C
D
E
F
G
H
I
J
K
L
M
N
O
P
Q
R
S
T
U
V
W
X
Y
Z

WIND WORLD

AREA	PASSWORD
1	0238
2	5943
3	6045
4	2850

Boss	8146

CLOUD WORLD

AREA	PASSWORD
1	9156
2	2715
3	4707
4	7046
Boss	0687

EVIL WORLD

AREA	PASSWORD
1	3725
2	0157
3	5826
4	9587
Boss	3752

Fight Only Bosses

Enter the password 9437 to play through boss stages back-to-back with all powerups.

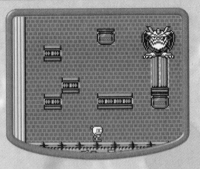

POWER QUEST

NATIONAL TOURNAMENT PASSWORD

Enter the following password:
P V 9 S
0 4 0 G
0 1 4 0

A B C D E F G H I J K L M N O P Q R S T U V W X Y Z

PREHISTORIK MAN

INVINCIBILITY AND LEVEL SELECT

During the introduction, press **Down, A, Up, B, Left, Right, B, A, B, A, B, A, Up, Down**. Press **SELECT** to skip levels.

PRINCE OF PERSIA

PASSWORDS

LEVEL	PASSWORD
2	06769075

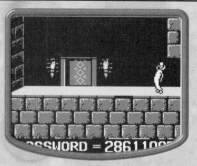

3	28611065
4	92117015
5	87019105
6	46308135
7	65903195
8	70914195
9	68813685
10	01414654

LEVEL	PASSWORD
11	32710744
12	26614774
Jaffar	98119464
Ending	89012414

Q*BERT

VIEW ALL MOVIES

At the Title Screen, press **Right, Up, B, A, Down, Up, B, Down, Up, B**.

QIX

NO SOUND

Hold Left and press START at the Title Screen.

A B C D E F G H I J K L M N O P Q R S T U V W X Y Z

R-TYPE

DE SOUZA EDITOR

At the High Score Screen, press **Down/Left + A + B.**

R-TYPE DX

DE SOUZA EDITOR

To unlock the De Souza Drawing Editor you mus beat R-Type, R-Type II and R-Type DX. Then, at the main menu, press right on the d-pad and the De Souza Editor option should appear.

INVULNERABILITY

Beat the DX Game mode on 10 credits or fewer, then in a non-DX game press Select+A to becom indestructible.

LEVEL SKIP

If you've already finished a stage, you can skip it by pressing B while the game is paused.

RAGING FIGHTER

PLAY AS SAME CHARACTER

Enter the following at the Title Screen:

MODE	CODE
1-player, same color	Up, Up, Down, Down, Left, Right, Left, Right, B, B
1-player, alternate color	Up, Up, Down, Down, Left, Right, Left, Right, B, A
2-player, same color	Up, Up, Down, Down, Left, Right, Left, Right, A, A
2-player, alternate color	Up, Up, Down, Down, Left, Right, Left, Right, A, B

RAMPAGE WORLD TOUR

2-PLAYER LINK MODE

To open up linked simultaneous play, go to the Options screen and **Hold Select, then press Up, Down, Left, Right, Down, Up.**

READY 2 RUMBLE BOXING

FIGHT AS KEMO CLAW

Highlight Arcade Mode and press Left (x3), Right (x3), Left, Right, Left, Right.

FIGHT AS NAT DADDY

Unlock Kemo Claw, highlight Arcade Mode, and press Right (x3), Left (x3), Right, Left, Right, Left.

FIGHT AS DAMIEN BLACK

Unlock Nat Daddy, highlight Arcade Mode, and press Right, Left, Right (x2), Left (x2), Right (x3), Left (x3).

REAL BOUT FATAL FURY SPECIAL

PLAY AS GEESE AND IORI

Defeat the game. Then press **START** on Billy and Krauser at the Player Select Screen.

SECRET OPTION

At the Options Screen, highlight Sound Test and press **Left + A**. You should have a new option, Soft Dip. Change the 0s to 1s.

A
B
C
D
E
F
G
H
I
J
K
L
M
N
O
P
Q
R
S
T
U
V
W
X
Y
Z

REAL GHOSTBUSTERS

PASSWORDS

LEVEL	PASSWORD
2	LFBD
3	VCSB
4	TRFF
5	ZFRG
6	NGSF
7	QDCZ
8	KCNG
9	TRBD
10	LGCK
11	WGRD
12	TCMF
13	RBCN
14	NBMF
15	GPBL
16	RBCT
17	RCNG
18	FCRF
19	YBRD
20	SGNG
21	GGLD
22	LBMP
23	TWCN
24	FDSF
25	SPGT
26	NFWS
27	RGSF
28	RBCF
29	DCSK
30	HBCR
31	JBZZ

LEVEL	PASSWORD
32	GBMF
33	HGLD
34	BCRD
35	DGLL
36	WGRM
37	STBR
40	HFLP
41	CTRL
42	FMHX
43	PCGR
44	LGSK
45	PRPY
46	NPTF
47	MSDP
48	MJCY
49	MFHD
50	CCNK
51	FNDG

ROAD RASH

PASSWORDS

LEVEL	PASSWORD
4	9DGG-BB9F-FFKK

```
ROAD RASH
ENTER PASSWORD

9DGG BB9F FFKK
LEVEL 4
ENTER NAME

PLAYER A
```

5	9CBK-632C-88K0

A B C D E F G H I J K L M N O P Q R S T U V W X Y Z

ROBOCOP 2

VIEW ENDING

At the Title Screen, press **A + B + SELECT + START**, then Left.

RUGRATS: THE MOVIE

PASSWORDS

LEVEL	PASSWORD
Train Crash	BVBYFJND

LEVEL	PASSWORD
Hospital	TQMMY QK
Light Woods	RJDBCVRT
Dark Woods	VNGBLJCV
Ancient Ruin	LJTBWQQD
Reptar	BJGSMVSH

SAMURAI SHODOWN 3

PLAY AS THE BOSSES

At the Takara Screen, press **SELECT** three times.

VIEW ENDINGS

At the Takara Screen, press **A, Up, B, Left, A, Down, B, Right**. After choosing a character, you will see his or her ending.

A
B
C
D
E
F
G
H
I
J
K
L
M
N
O
P
Q
R
S
T
U
V
W
X
Y
Z

SHADOWGATE CLASSIC

SURVIVE FIRE WITHOUT A CLOAK

To proceed through areas too hot to survive, follow these steps. Enter the room as normal, and the unbearable heat will immediately render you unconscious. You will wake in the Mirrored Room; touch one of the wall mirrors. You will be killed instantly, but if you continue you will find yourself in the hot room without feeling the ill effects of the fire.

SHANGHAI

SPECIAL MODES

During a game, press **SELECT** to get the Options Menu. Highlight New Game and press **A**. You can now enter the following:

CODE	EFFECT
ZAP	Zap sound effect
STF	Credits
MAN	Fewer tiles
REV	Tile turns over when selected

SKATE OR DIE: TOUR DE THRASH

PASSWORDS

LEVEL	PASSWORD
2	GNBF
3	MTGP
4	PVFS
5	FVCH
6	BXHN
7	GFTQ
8	JZWC

SMALL SOLDIERS

PASSWORDS

LEVEL	PASSWORD
4	Archer, Brick, Kip, Chip
5	Kip, Chip, Archer, Brick

SMURFS

PASSWORDS

LEVEL	PASSWORD
5	pbsp
10	zrms

A B C D E F G H I J K L M N O P Q R S T U V W X Y Z

THE SMURFS' NIGHTMARE

PASSWORDS

LEVEL	PASSWORD
2	Glasses, Pencil, Mouth
3	Soap Bubble, Mouth, Glasses

SOCCER MANIA

INVISIBLE OPPONENT

Press **Up, Up, Down, Down, Left, Right, Left, Right, B, A, START** at the Title Screen.

SPACE INVADERS

CLASSIC MODE

Enter the password CLSS1281999DBM.

PASSWORDS

LEVEL	PASSWORD
1 Venus	RTJN PBKC X2RJPW
2 Earth	WWYX TC2N QW79VY
3 Mars	?WZ4 VCLN 4W81V?
4 Jupiter	RSSN 3QJ7 8?GJMC
5 Saturn	WSPZ MSO8 N?H8NF
6 Uranus	CV1? QWKG J3X8R5
7 Neptune	HV27 RW1G N3YOR7
8 Pluto	MV7H RCLH S3ZSR9
9 Alien Homeworld	RV8R RC2H X3?RJC

SPANKY'S QUEST

STAGE SELECT
Enter the password **0119**.

SOUND TEST
Enter the password **0117**.

SPAWN

PASSWORDS
Chapter 6: Heart, Skull, Spawn, Spawn
Chapter 7: Skull, Spawn, Spawn, Heart

SPEEDY GONZALES

PASSWORDS

LEVEL	PASSWORD
Mexico	500999
Forest	343003
Desert	830637
Country	812171
Island	522472

SPUDS ADVENTURE

STAGE SELECT
Enter the password **BANCHOU**.

SPY VS. SPY

LEVEL SELECT
Enter the password **15Y24**.

SPY VS. SPY: OPERATION BOOBY TRAP

PASSWORDS

STAGE	PASSWORD
6	ZKP
11	YPT
16	MMD

STAR TREK: 25TH ANNIVERSARY

PASSWORDS

LEVEL	PASSWORD
First Planet	0523.4
Second System	7552.3
Second Planet	6541.2
Third System	5570.1
Third Planet	4567.0
Last System	3516.7

STAR TREK GENERATIONS: BEYOND THE NEXUS

PASSWORDS

STAGE	PASSWORD
2	HARRIMAN
3	DEMORA
4	SOREN
5	VERIDIAN
6	OGAWA
7	FARRAGUT

STAR TREK: THE NEXT GENERATION

LEVEL SELECT

Enter the password **Override**.

PASSWORDS

RANK	PASSWORD
Ensign	Q
Lieutenant	Barclay
Lt. Commander	Tomalak
Commander	Ro Laren
Captain	Locutus

A B C D E F G H I J K L M N O P Q R S T U V W X Y Z

PASSWORDS

LEVEL	PASSWORD
Dance Hall	SNKMTD
Sail Barge	RWVJBC
Endor	TFGBMN

Ewok Village	HJMKPL
Power Generator	QGTHGD
Death Star	PSVZKL
Tower	SFPYSW
Death: Mission 2	KFGZXQ

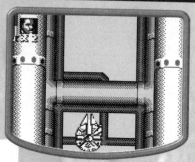

SUMO FIGHTER

PASSWORDS

2-1	532773
3-1	355530
4-1	524358
5-1	650594
2-2	753442
3-2	526158
4-2	780554
5-2	105960
2-3	362459
3-3	085530
4-3	546127
5-3	155965
Final	968158

SUPER MARIO BROS. DX

"You Vs. Boo" Race Levels

Get 100,000 pts. in one "normal" game to access these head-to-head stages.

Unlock "SMB For Super Players"

Get 300,000 pts. in one "normal" game to unlock Super Mario Bros. For Super Players. This is the same as the Japanese SMB 2/Super Mario: The Lost Levels, except that Luigi is not available. (Instead, Mario has Luigi's higher jumping abilities.)

A
B
C
D
E
F
G
H
I
J
K
L
M
N
O
P
Q
R
S
T
U
V
W
X
Y
Z

Level Select

When you beat the game once, you can select your starting point.

Yoshi Egg Finder in Challenge Mode

Once you've found at least one Yoshi Egg, a Yoshi option should appear in the Toy Box. Select it, and a random level's Egg location will be shown. At first, it only shows the screen you should find the egg on, but as you get more eggs, the hints become more detailed.

Album Pictures

To get all the album pictures, do the following:

Page 1:	(Top-Left) Fill up the Score Meter in Challenge
	(Top-Right) Get every medal in Challenge
	(Middle) Beat Original Mode
	(Bottom Left) Beat all the Star Levels in Original
	(Bottom Right) Beat SMB For Super Players
Page 2:	(Top Left) Get the end-of-level Fireworks
	(Top Middle) Get a 1-Up Mushroom
	(Top Right) Find and climb a Bonus Stage Vine
	(Middle Left) Beat Original 1985 Mode
	(Middle) Save the Princess
	(Middle Right) Use the link cable to trade High Scores
	(Bottom Left) Get every Red Coin medal in Challenge

	(Bottom Middle) Get every High Score medal in Challenge	A
	(Bottom Right) Get every Yoshi Egg in Challenge	B
age 3:	(Top Left) Kill a Little Goomba	C
	(Top Middle) Kill a Bloober	D
	(Top Right) Kill Lakitu	E
	(Middle Left) Kill a Cheep Cheep	F
	(Middle) Kill a Hammer Brother	G
	(Middle Right) Kill a Bullet Bill	H
	(Bottom Left) Kill a Koopa Troopa	I
	(Bottom Middle) Kill a Spiny	J
	(Bottom Right) Kill a Buzzy Beetle	
age 4:	(Top Left) Kill Bowser in World 1 with fireballs	K
	(Top Right) Kill Bowser in World 2 with fireballs	L
	(Bottom Left) Kill Bowser in World 3 with fireballs	M
	(Bottom Right) Kill Bowser in World 4 with fireballs	N
age 5:	(Top Left) Kill Bowser in World 5 with fireballs	O
	(Top Right) Kill Bowser in World 6 with fireballs	P
	(Bottom Left) Kill Bowser in World 7 with fireballs	Q
	(Bottom Right) Kill Bowser in World 8 with fireballs	R

S
T
U
V
W
X
Y
Z

SUPER MARIO LAND 2: 6 GOLDEN COINS

EASIER GAME

Press **SELECT** at the Pipe Screen.

PLAY THE DEMOS

DEMO	CODE
1	Up + SELECT
2	Up + A + SELECT
3	Up + B + SELECT
4	Up + A + B + SELECT

TARZAN

PASSWORDS

LEVEL	PASSWORD
2-1	4-2-3-4
3-1	1-1-5-6
4-1	2-3-7-4
5-1	7-7-3-1
6-1	6-5-4-7

TAZ-MANIA

PASSWORDS

LEVEL	PASSWORD
2	345371
3	745577
4	367123
5	662077

TECMOBOWL

CHAMPIONSHIP GAME PASSWORDS

GAME	PASSWORD
San Fransisco vs. Denver	1DAFF7A6
L.A. vs. Washington	967FBFA5
Washington vs. Chicago	587BFFA0
Indianapolis vs. L.A.	438FDFAD
Chicago vs. L.A.	A89FDFA8
Miami vs. San Fransisco	072F7FAA
Dallas vs. San Fransisco	202F7FAE
Denver vs. L.A.	0C8FDFA9
Cleveland vs. New York	098DFFA9
Minnesota vs. L.A.	2E9FDEA3
Seattle vs. Washington	937FBFA5
New York vs. Miami	24AFFDAD
L.A. vs. Miami	94BFFDAI
Invisible Team vs. Chicago	397BFFA5

A
B
C
D
E
F
G
H
I
J
K
L
M
N
O
P
Q
R
S
T
U
V
W
X
Y
Z

MIRROR IMAGE TEAM PASSWORDS

TEAM	PASSWORD
Washington	5B7FBFA3
Indianapolis	43AFFEAC
Cleveland	49AFFBA9
San Fransisco	9C3F7FA5
Chicago	697BFFA5
Minnesota	AC#&FFA9
Denver	CFBFF7A0
Miami	46AFFDAB
L.A.	969FDFA5
Dallas	63AEFFA5
N.Y.	269DFFA1

TEENAGE MUTANT NINJA TURTLES: FALL OF THE FOOT CLAN

RESTORE LIFE

Pause the game and press **Up, Up, Down, Down, Left, Right, Left, Right, B, A**. This code will work only once per game.

PRACTICE THE BONUS GAMES

At the Title Screen, hold **A + B + SELECT** and press **START**. At the Stage Select Screen, select the question mark.

TEENAGE MUTANT NINJA TURTLES 3: RADICAL RESCUE

PASSWORDS

LEVEL	PASSWORD
Before Scratch	1000002
After Scratch	2100002
After Card 1	4110102

Before Dirtbag	1111102
After Dirtbag	2311102
After Raphael	3311302

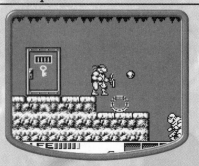

After Card 2	4331302
Before Triceraton	1311302
After Triceraton	2711302
After Donatello	3711702
After Card 3	4773702
Before Scale Tail	1777702
After Scale Tail	2H77702
After Splinter	3H77H02
After Card 4	4HH7H02
Before Shredder	1HHHH02

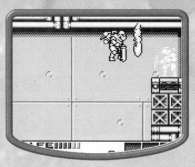

A
B
C
D
E
F
G
H
I
J
K
L
M
N
O
P
Q
R
S
T
U
V
W
X
Y
Z

TENNIS

EASY WIN

When you serve, toss the ball and let it hit you in the head. This should give you the point.

TETRIS

HARDER GAME

At the Title Screen, hold **Down** and press **START**.

NO PREVIEW

Pause the game and press **SELECT**.

TETRIS 2

EASIER GAME

At the Title Screen, press and hold **Up + START** until the Title Screen disappears.

TETRIS ATTACK

EXTRA PUZZLES

Enter the password **JO!JOO6O**.

FIGHT BOWSER

Enter the password **78RN5B?8**.

PASSWORDS FOR HARD MODE

LEVEL	PASSWORD
2	?4XJ70ON
3	?28J71HN
4	Q1LK51ZN
5	CCK82TP
6	!WML12!P
7	PZ5LQCZP
8	KJXMJXXP
9	YKHMJYWP
10	ZPPM5YWP
11	RN9NRZUP

SUPER HARD GAME

On Vs. Com Mode, highlight Hard then hold
Up + SELECT, A or START.

A
B
C
D
E
F
G
H
I
J
K
L
M
N
O
P
Q
R
S
T
U
V
W
X
Y
Z

TETRIS BLAST

DIFFERENT MUSIC

Pause the game and press **SELECT** to change the music.

FIGHT MODE

At the Main Menu, press **B (x5), START**.

PASSWORDS

LEVEL	PASSWORD
2	ZFFFJJJF
3	B/MMLLKB
4	XSDDGGDM
5	KCWGLLHK
6	VG.LJJDM
7	K.TDGGMF
8	XZSCDDKK
9	DFMYLLDD
10	YGCPDDHL
11	GVMYLLCJ
12	V/JVDDGK
13	CJXTBBCF
14	!L.YLKKL
15	LXWTBMMB
16	VSRPDCCH
17	KBCDTFDF
18	XDFGYKJF
19	F!CDTFCM
20	TTGHPMJB
21	DBVGYKGD
22	.JRCRCKB

LEVEL	PASSWORD
23	CY/BPMHF
28	?!JWTFJK
29	FKWTP-MDH
31	LVRPRCFG
32	VS.YYKMF
33	MGFGLYLF
46	ZCYXJVMH

TETRIS DX

WALL-CRAWLING BLOCKS

A bug in Tetris DX allows for irregular blocks (not 4-bars or squares) to be pushed back up the well. Hold **Left** or **Right** until the piece is pressing against the wall. Continue to hold the direction and quickly, repeatedly rotate the piece with **A** for the left wall and **B** for the right wall. The block will climb up the wall slowly.

TINY TOON ADVENTURES: MONTANA'S MOVIE MADNESS

TOUGHER GAME

At the Title Screen, press **A** + **START**.

OPTIONS MENU

At the Title Screen, press **B** + **START**.

SUB GAMES

Before the Konami Screen, hold **A** + **B**. At the Press START Screen, press **START** while still holding **A** + **B**.

A B C D E F G H I J K L M N O P Q R S T U V W X Y Z

TINY TOON ADVENTURES: WACKY SPORTS

EVENT SELECT

At the Title Screen, press **Up, Up, Down, Down, Left, Right, Left, Right, B, A, START**.

TOM & JERRY FRANTIC ANTIC

PASSWORDS

LEVEL PASSWORD

Level 5	Fish, Star, Cracker, Potato, Hea
Level 9	Heart, Heart, Watermelon, Watermelon, Fish

TOP GEAR POCKET

ALL CARS AND COURSES

Enter the password **YQXW_H**.

ALL GOLD TROPHIES

Enter the password **YQX_%Z**.
Nine Cars and Six Tracks
Enter the password **TWX+%Z** to get a head start smaller than the ones above.

TOP GUN: GUTS AND GLORY

PASSWORDS

LEVEL	PASSWORD
2	WN7WQQT
3	8NQSQQL
4	PNQZQQP
5	KNKQWQQ
6	CN4XWQQ
7	SN7TWQP
8	XN778Q4
9	7N7FPQF
10	FN2FKQF

TOY STORY 2

LEVEL	PASSWORD
2	PBPP
3	BJWJ
4	PJBW
5	WBPP
6	JBPJ
7	JJWW
8	PBWJ
9	BPWW

A
B
C
D
E
F
G
H
I
J
K
L
M
N
O
P
Q
R
S
T
U
V
W
X
Y
Z

TRUE LIES

SECRET LEVEL

Enter the password **RSSHLS**.

TUROK: BATTLE OF THE BIONOSAURS

PASSWORDS

LEVEL	PASSWORD
2	GRZNNPCRDB
3	DVZNDPBTNG
4	GVZNDPBTNG
5	PCVYGRBTDK
6	RCVYGRSTDR
7	VSVYTRSQDG
8	RSQPTNSQNW

TUROK: RAGE WARS

LEVEL	EASY	MEDIUM	HARD
2	K14QF4	3MQTL1	DT5JV1
3	3T5L31	Z1KMQ1	2F5QZM
4	SMJ54M	2TQCMR	MQ5LRS

TUROK 2: SEEDS OF EVIL

INFINITE WEAPONS
Enter the password **DLVTRKBWPS**.

BIRD MODE
Enter the password **DLVTRKBBRD**.

INFINITE LIVES
Enter the password **DLVTRKBLVS**.

INFINITE ENERGY
Enter the password **DLVTRKBNRG**.

PASSWORDS

LEVEL	PASSWORD
2	DVYLWKVYTQ
3	GRYLWKWVCZ
4	DRYLSRWVZN
5	GVZLSRWQLS
6	DVZLBVSQLN
7	GRZLBVBQLL
8	DRZLBVBQLN
9	GVYNBVBQGD

LEVEL SKIP
Enter the password **DLVTRKBLVL**.

ALTERNATE ENDING
On Level 9, when the stage's sole enemy appears press **DOWN** to enter a secret tunnel. Blast the computer and incubator therein to view a different ending sequence.

A
B
C
D
E
F
G
H
I
J
K
L
M
N
O
P
Q
R
S
T
U
V
W
X
Y
Z

TURRICAN

INVINCIBILITY

At the Title Screen, press **A, B, B, A, B, A, A, B, A, A, B, A, A**. You can skip a stage by pausing the game and pressing **SELECT**.

LEVEL SELECT

At the Title Screen, hold **SELECT** and press **START**.

TWOUBLE

PASSWORDS

Granny's House 1: Dog, Granny, Tweety, Taz, Sylvester

Granny's Cellar 1: Taz, Sylvester, Tweety, Dog, Granny

Garden 1: Sylvester, Tweety, Dog, Taz, Granny

Streets 1: Dog, Tweety, Taz, Granny, Sylvester

Toy Store 1: Taz, Dog, Tweety, Sylvester, Granny

URBAN STRIKE

PASSWORDS

LEVEL	PASSWORD
Baja Oil Rigs	M72D20QHTB5
Mexico	FD4LHQQ93DJ

V-RALLY CHAMPIONSHIP EDITION

PASSWORDS IN ARCADE MODE

DIFFICULTY	PASSWORD
Medium	FAST
Hard	FOOD

WARIO BLAST

ALL POWER-UPS

To get all power-ups as Bomberman, enter the password **4622**. To get all power-ups as Wario, enter the password **2264**.

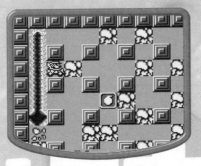

BOMBERMAN PASSWORDS

ROUND	PASSWORD
1-1	4696
1-2	7006
1-3	8774
1 Boss	5141
2-1	9185
2-2	4610
2-3	2630
2 Boss	3569
3-1	8401
3-2	8264
3-3	0173
3 Boss	2828
4-1	4152
4-2	3451
4-3	4312
4 Boss	0874
5-1	1909
5-2	5010
5-3	2904
5 Boss	1726
6-1	3614
6-2	0610
6-3	9867
6 Boss	9618
7-1	1884
7-2	7702
7-3	6925
7 Boss	7110

ROUND	PASSWORD
8-1	5814
8-2	8136
8-3	0390
8 Boss	3158

WARIO PASSWORDS

ROUND	PASSWORD
1-1	6964
1-2	6007
1-3	4778
1 Boss	1415
2-1	5819
2-2	0164
2-3	0362
2 Boss	9653
3-1	1048
3-2	4628
3-3	3710
3 Boss	8282
4-1	2514
4-2	1543
4-3	2134
4 Boss	4780
5-1	9091
5-2	0105
5-3	4092
5 Boss	6271

A
B
C
D
E
F
G
H
I
J
K
L
M
N
O
P
Q
R
S
T
U
V
W
X
Y
Z

ROUND	PASSWORD
6-1	4163
6-2	0160
6-3	7689
6 Boss	8169
7-1	4881
7-2	2077
7-3	5296
7 Boss	0117
8-1	4185
8-2	6318
8-3	0930
8 Boss	8513

SECRET BATTLE GAME

Enter the password **5656** to play as
Bomberman, or **6565** to play as Wario.

WARIO LAND:
SUPER MARIO LAND 3

DEBUG MODE

Pause the game and press **SELECT 16
times.** A box should appear on the lives. Hold
B and press **Left or Right** to select a number
to change. Press **Up or Down** to change the
number.

WAYNE'S WORLD

LEVEL SKIP

Pause the game, hold **B + A** and press **Left, Left, SELECT**.

PROGRAMMER'S FRIEND

During game play, hold **START** and press **Right, A, Down, A, Right, B, Right, A.**

PROGRAMMER'S GIRLFRIEND

During game play, hold **START** and press **SELECT, A, Left, A, Down, Left, A, SELECT, SELECT.**

A
B
C
D
E
F
G
H
I
J
K
L
M
N
O
P
Q
R
S
T
U
V
W
X
Y
Z

PROGRAMMER'S PICTURE

During game play, hold **START** and press **A, B**
A, Down, Left, A, Down.

WHO FRAMED
ROGER RABBIT?

PASSWORDS

LEVEL	PASSWORD
2	DLT3QYBY
3	GPLDMSRC
4	MMCFGWXJ
5	BGQTVKJP
6	RTJBWN43

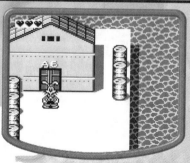

WIZARDS AND WARRIORS CHAPTER X: THE FORTRESS OF FEAR

SIX LIVES

Finish a game and enter **W, Heart, W** at the High Score Screen.

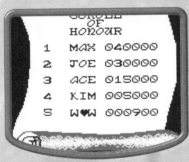

```
        SCROLL
         OF
       HONOUR
  1  MAX  040000
  2  JOE  030000
  3  ACE  015000
  4  KIM  005000
  5  W♥W  000900
```

WORLD HEROES 2 JET

SCORCHER MODE

Press **Right, Left, A, B, Down, A, B, Up** at the Takara logo. You should hear a sound if entered correctly. This allows you to use your super attack at any time, select a fighting style in Tournament Mode, and select Zeus.

JET MODE

At the Title Screen, press **Up, Up, SELECT, A, Down, Down SELECT, B**. You should hear a sound if entered correctly.

A B C D E F G H I J K L M N O P Q R S T U V W X Y Z

WWF ATTITUDE

JARRETT PASSWORDS

OPPONENT	PASSWORD
Triple H	LGJCRMHG
Shamrock	PKHDSNJK
Val Venis	NJGFTPKJ
Steve Austin	RCFGLQBC
Gangrel	QBDHMRCB
The Rock	TFCJNSDF
Road Dogg	SDBKPTFD
Mankind	CRTLGBQR
Sable	BQSMHCRQ
Kane	FTRNJDST
Goldust	DSQPKFTS
X Pac	HMPQBGLM
Bossman	GLNRCHML

STONE COLD STEVE AUSTIN PASSWORDS

OPPONENT	PASSWORD
Gangrel	CBFPCQJC
Sable	BCDNBRKB
Jarrett	FDCMFSGF
Undertaker	RQTKRBNR
Road Dogg	QRSJQCPQ
The Rock	TSRHTDLT
Bossman	STQGSFMS
Goldust	LPFMGSM
Taka	LMNDLHTL
Al Snow	PNMCPJQP
Billy Gunn	PLBNKRN
Val Venis	HQKTHLDH
Edge	GRJSGMFG
X-Pac	KSHRKNBK

THE ROCK CAREER MODE PASSWORDS

VICTORIES	OPPONENT	PASSWORD
1	Road Dogg	GHKRCSCG
2	Taka	KJGSDRDK
3	Triple H	JKHPFRFJ
4	Bossman	CBDQGNGC
5	Godfather	BCFRHPHB
6	Shamrock	ZFDBSJLJF
7	Austin	DFCTKMKD
8	Edge	RQSBLJLR
9	Val Venis	QRTCMKMQ
10	Al Snow	TSQDNGNT
11	X-Pac	STRFPHPS
12	Billy Gunn	LNGQDQM
15	Kane	NPMKTCTN
16	Mankind	HQJLBSBH
17	Goldust	GRKMCTCG
18	Gangrel	KSGNDQDK

WWF SUPERSTARS 2

FIGHT OUTSIDE RING

At the Ring Select Screen, press **A, B, Up, Down, Left, Right, START**.

A
B
C
D
E
F
G
H
I
J
K
L
M
N
O
P
Q
R
S
T
U
V
W
X
Y
Z

WWF WARZONE

FINISHING MOVES

WRESTLER	MOVE NAME	MOVE
Shawn Michaels	Sweet Chin Music	Hold Special, Left Right, Up
Kane	Tombstone Piledriver	Hold Special, Right, Up, Down
Ken Shamrock	Ankle Lock Submission	Hold Special, Left Up, Right
Steve Austin	Stone Cold Stunner	Hold Special, Down, Left, Right
Faarooq	The Dominator	Hold Special, Down, Up, Left
Goldust	Curtain Call	Hold Special, Right, Down, Right
Triple H	The Pedigree	Hold Special, Up, Left, Down
Mankind	Mandible Claw	Hold Special, Up, Right, Left (Over a Fallen Opponent)
Owen Hart	Spinning Heel Kick	Hold Special, Down, Right, Left
The Rock	The Rock Bottom	Hold Special, Left, Down, Up
British Bulldog	Running Powerslam	Hold Special, Right, Left, Down
Ahmed Johnson	Pearl River Plunge	Hold Special, Up, Down, Left
The Undertaker	Tombstone Piledriver	Hold Special, Left, Down, Right

STONE COLD STEVE AUSTIN'S PASSWORDS

RANK	PASSWORD
12	JGTCDGK
11 (Feud)	HKQFCKG
11	RKQFCTG
10	JJRFBJH
9	CCNHKCD
8	DGFHJBF
7 (Feud)	CKBKHFB
7	MKBKHPB
6	DJCKGDC
5 (Feud)	RMSMPRS
4	SQTMNQT
3 (Feud)	RTQPMTQ
2	SSRPLSR

A
B
C
D
E
F
G
H
I
J
K
L
M
N
O
P
Q
R
S
T
U
V
W
X
Y
Z

KANE'S PASSWORDS

RANK	PASSWORD
12	JHRFOHK
11 (Feud)	HJSCKJG
11	RJSCKSG
10	JKTCJKH
9	CBLKCBD
8	DHCKBCF
7 (Feud)	CJDHFDB
7	MJDHFNB
6	DKFHDFC
5	RLQPRQS
4 (Feud)	SRRPQRT
4 (IC Title)	JRRPQHT
3 (Feud)	RSSMTSQ
3	HSSMTJQ
2	STTMSTR

MANKIND'S PASSWORDS

RANK	PASSWORD
12	DHRFDGJ
11	CJSCCKH
10 (Feud)	DKTCBJG
10	NKTCBSG
9	HBLKKCF
8	JHCKJBD

RANK	PASSWORD
7 (Feud)	HJDHHFC
7	RJDHHPC
6	JKFHGDB
5	MLQPPRT
4	NRRPNQS
3 (Feud)	MSSMMTR
3	CSSMMKR

TRIPLE H'S PASSWORDS

RANK	PASSWORD
12	DGSHDHG
11	CKRKCJK
10 (Feud)	DJQKBKJ
9	HCPCKBC
8 (Feud)	JGDCJCB
7	HKCFHDF
6	JJBFGFD
5	MMTRPQR
4 (Feud)	NQSRNRQ
3 (Feud)	MTRTMST
2	NSQTLTS

A
B
C
D
E
F
G
H
I
J
K
L
M
N
O
P
Q
R
S
T
U
V
W
X
Y
Z

UNDERTAKER'S PASSWORDS

RANK	CODE
7 (Feud)	HSCFKDD
7	RSCFKND
6	JTBFJFF
5	MBTRMQQ
4 (Feud)	NHSRLRR
4	DHSRLHR
3 (Feud)	MJRTPSS

YOSHI'S COOKIE

EXTRA LEVELS

Set the Music Type to Off, the Speed to Hi. Highlight Round, hold **Up** and press **SELECT**.

GAME BOY® LEGAL LINES

Game Boy® is a registered trademark of Nintendo of America Inc.

A BUG'S LIFE ©1998 Disney. All rights reserved. ©1998 THQ. Inc. THQ is a registered trademark of THQ, Inc.

THE ADDAMS FAMILY 2: PUGSLEY'S SCAVENGER HUNT ™ ©1992 Paramount Pictures. ©1992 H-B Production Co. Based on the characters created by Charles Addams. Licensing agent Paramount Pictures.

ADVENTURE ISLAND ©1991 Hudson Soft. All rights reserved.

ADVENTURE ISLAND II © HUDSON SOFT. Licensed to Nintendo. ™ and ® are trademarks of Nintendo of America, Inc.

AFTER BURST ©1990 NCS. All rights reserved.

ALADDIN ©1993 The Walt Disney Company ©1994 Virgin Interactive Entertainment. All rights reserved.

AMAZING PENGUIN and AMAZING TATER © Atlus Sofware, Inc. All rights reserved.

ANIMANIACS ©1995 Konami Co, Ltd. Animaniacs, characters, names and all related indicia are trademarks of Warner Bros. ©1995 Program ©1995 Factor 5.

THE ATOMIC PUNK ©1991 Hudson Soft. All rights reserved.

BATMAN ©1939 DC Comics, Inc. All rights reserved. ©1990 Sunsoft.

BATMAN FOREVER Batman and all related elements are property of DC Comics ™ and ©1995, All rights reserved. ©1995 Acclaim Entertainment, Inc.

BATTLE ARENA TOSHINDEN is a trademark of Takara, Inc. ©1996 by Takara, Inc. All rights reserved.

BATTLE BULL ©1990 Seta. All rights reserved.

BATTLE PINGPONG ©1990 Quest. All rights reserved.

BATTLESHIP is a trademark and © 1992 Milton Bradley Co., a division of Hasbro Inc. ©1992 Use Corp. All Rights Reserved. Licensed by Mindscape, Inc.